Kitchen Existential
Restaurant Chefs in Their Own Words

By Halliwell Hobbes
Author of *Restaurants: Bite-Size Observations about the Last Civilized Places on Earth*

COPYRIGHT NOTICE

Printed in the United States of America.

"Often, admiring a chef and then getting to know him is like loving goose liver and then meeting the goose."

— George Lang

MR. ANGELO CAREFULLY GUARDING AS MUCH AS POSSIBLE HIS SECRET RECIPE NOT TO LET EVEN HIS EMPLOYEES KNOW HIS SECRET FORMULAS AS TO THEIR PREPARATIONS GULFPORT. MISS.

Eat These Words

Hypothetical Question: What would happen if you put 100 of the world's finest chefs all in one room and started a conversation about their profession?

Answer: You would get the bracing and invigorating rhetorical exchange found in this book.

Fasten your apron strings, *Kitchen Existential* is a rollicking roller-coaster ride, an entertaining, enlightening, back-of-the-house view of the high-stakes world of the restaurant chef — offered in delectable, bite-size portions, peppered liberally with wit and insight.

Think of this opuscule -- a delicious confection in its own right -- as a sampling of opinions and perspectives acquired in a world where stockpots boil, sauté pans sizzle, and tempers often run hot during the long hours of intense stress and painstaking attention to detail. You are certain to find pearls of wisdom courtesy of the people who turn mealtimes into opportunities for delight and surprise -- on the mastery of food and flavor, preparing and sharing, on the culinary profession and hospitality industry. It's guaranteed to reveal a few things you never knew about chefs at the top of their culinary craft.

Just enough to whet your appetite.

"This is one of the hardest professions that there is anywhere. It looks very glamorous but at the end of the day you are peeling onions, cutting tomatoes, washing dishes, and getting blood on your hands. That is the truth. It's not glamorous, but at the same time that's exactly what makes it so exciting."

— José Andres

"My philosophy has always been the same: start with sustainable, organic ingredients and apply both modern and classic technique. Obviously I say local, sustainable, and organic for one reason — I can't commit to only one of the three categories because you can't sustain a restaurant in the mid-Atlantic all year serving all local product. It wouldn't be right. I decided that I can't change the world, so at least we are making an impact by being as responsible as possible."

— Bryan Voltaggio

"I enjoy the art and the actual physical aspect of cooking. Whatever I do, I want to be sure that I never separate myself from the actual physical part of being a chef."

— Eli Kaimeh

"In a famous restaurant, you were more likely to know who the maître d' was than the chef. That's really changed now, and we have Wolfgang Puck to thank for that."

— Rick Bayless

"Our trade is becoming less blue-collar, and that challenges us to rethink and change our trade for the better."

— René Redzepi

"Being a great chef today is not enough – you have to be a great businessman."

— Wolfgang Puck

"Cooking is drifting away from the 'essential' into the artificial. To me, food is the best symbol of exchange: it's an act of sharing around a table. One should not forget that, and we should go back to this concept of exchange and sharing."

— Michel Bras

"Restaurants shouldn't just be about the chef;
it should be an experience."

— Bill Telepan

"When you are cooking, you have to think of
who is eating the things you will cook. You
are doing it to give pleasure to someone else,
not to yourself."

— Stevie Parle

"I'm more interested in flavor and ingredients than technique. Technique is secondary to us. It's more about the seasons and how something tastes. Without those, you don't have a foundation to stand on. You can only manipulate something so much and make it seem like something it's not."

— Curtis Duffy

"I am of a new generation of American chefs who find stimulation in sharing ideas with and learning from chefs and cooks from my own and other cultures and in talking with those who know and care about food, then incorporating what I've learned into my own personal style of cuisine."

— Dean Fearing

"Cooking is a great way to express yourself. If you're not in a good mood, if things aren't in harmony, it will show."

— Marcus Samuelsson

"Interesting is not enough. Food must be pleasurable and delicious."

— Paul Liebrandt

"We are not a church or a temple of anything. We are a restaurant where people come to have an experience."

— Eric Ripert

"My one unbreakable rule has always been to use only the freshest and finest ingredients available."

— Alice Waters

"I really admire everybody who's in this business, because culinary arts is one of the hardest businesses to be in. It's also very rewarding, because you look at somebody eating, and they're smiling."

— Jean-Georges Vongerichten

"The difference between a technical cuisine that can be easily reproduced, and a really creative cuisine is the emotion your pour into the food."

— Alain Ducasse

"You can't beat the feeling of venturing out-doors and picking a few ingredients from the garden to cook with."

— Gordon Ramsay

"I think one of the reasons why certain restaurants are extremely successful is because they have a way of conveying to people that they're in a certain place, whether it's through the produce they use, the technique, or the ideology of the food they're serving."

— Mourad Lahlou

"Food, years ago, was at the bottom of the social scale. Any good mother would have wanted their child to marry a lawyer, a doctor, an architect — certainly not a cook! Now we are geniuses."

— Jacques Pepin

"Gastronomy is the art to lift an ingredient or recipe to its best moment."

— Alex Atala

"I don't think you can get into this business without having some experience at culinary school. It teaches you the basics, which are the fundamental tools in our industry, the basic principles of cooking, preparation, organization, menu terminology and understanding. Without those basic elements I don't think you can build a successful career. It's like everything in life; you have to have a great foundation in order to build on it."

— Michael Bonacini

"My inspiration comes from the fact that I love food and I love people. I always have. And I've always been around food. I started washing dishes at the age of 14 and from that young age, I knew what I wanted to do."

— Ned Bell

"Listen to the ingredients; treat them with finesse, and they're happy."

— José Andres

"I was a punk. I submitted myself to washing dishes before I learned to chop. I learned how to wash pots and pans before I learned to cook."

— Alex Atala

"Meat and fish are just like a dressing. The main thing is the vegetables."

— Rodrigo de la Calle

"Practice, practice, practice. Just keep baking, because you don't get good at something by doing it once."

— Michelle Gayer

"About 10 or 15 years ago our palates woke up. Most of our food was European and English, which is the most bland on the planet. We are definitely a melting pot of culture. We are passionate about exploring food of other countries."

— Rick Bayless

"A chef should take nutrition seriously. You're giving someone sustenance. If you think, 'I don't care if my customers live or die, so what shortcuts can I take?' then just go do something else."

— Lenny Russo

"If you understand French cooking, you can cook anything."

— Kevin Kohler

"Wherever there's good agriculture, there's also really good food."

— Rick Bayless

"When I was 13, I realized that the kitchen would be my playground, my hobby, and my profession."

— Wolfgang Puck

"When I was younger, I saw all these guys opening all these restaurants and I thought, why not me? Now I think, why me? I just wanted to cook good meals and make people smile."

— Michel Richard

"Food should be delicious. When you go to a restaurant, it is to have a great experience with friends and family. I go to the market and am inspired by different foods that I find there. I love [using] different textures; there might be an interesting vegetable or fish, or anything new that catches my eye."

— Chef Michel Richard

"I think the best meal of your life is made by the company that you share it with. That will always make even a bad dinner pretty good, because when you leave you'll have had more than just food; you've had a life experience."

— Eli Kaimeh

"I think the most wonderful thing in the world is another chef. I'm always excited about learning new things about food."

— Paul Prudhomme

"Familiarity is important. We always use familiar items, ingredients, components, and pairings."

— Shea Gallante

"A cook's cook is a person who is so dedicated to his craft, and so much more interested in how to roast a piece of meat than being on television."

— Tien Ho

"Like most chefs or people in the business, you have some frenetic energy inside you all the time."

— Andrew Carmellini

"Just like if you were brought up on a farm, you would most likely carry on your father's business as a farmer; I was brought up in the kitchen and ended up becoming a chef."

— Martin Yan

"A jazz musician can improvise based on his knowledge of music. He understands how things go together. For a chef, once you have that basis, that's when cuisine is truly exciting."

— Charlie Trotter

"Cooking is the art of adjustment."

— Jacques Pépin

"A meal is a dialogue between a cook and the people who will be eating it."

— Rick Bayless

"There are many trends but I'm not interested in trends. I am interested in things that are here to stay."

— José Andres

"Could you imagine people eating a painting — if they could introduce a painting into their bodies? It's probably the artist's dream, and we have the opportunity to do so."

— Ferran Adrià

"Many people say that Italian food, and some-times the food we make, is so simple. The reality is, it's so hard to execute that. There's nothing to hide behind..... You have to make sure to execute it perfectly every time. That's the hard part about our food, and what makes it so interesting."

— Marc Vetri

"One piece of advice I offer young cooks is to choose their mentors wisely. It's probably because mine were so influential in my life. From the start, I worked for the best chefs who would hire me and then gave them my all. In each case, they repaid me by in turn introducing me to yet another great mentor."

— Daniel Boulud

"Cooking in a restaurant is not creative; it's manufacturing — making it right every time."

— Sang Yoon

"I look at a work of art and get an inspiration for mixing colors of food. I see a design and can envision a pattern on the plate."

— Marcus Samuelsson

"I learned more from the one restaurant that didn't work than from all the ones that were successes."

— Wolfgang Puck

"We stopped bringing food from the other side of the world a long time ago. Buying locally conserves flavor and creates demanding jobs."

— Alain Ducasse

"We are a country that is ready to throw off the shackles of the European domination of cooking. We don't feel we need to learn only European ways of cooking. America is opening up to learn that there is more out there than French cooking. We have thrown off those shackles."

— Rick Bayless

"I see myself as a craftsman and absolutely not an artist. I like the produce: I have a very close relationship to the produce and ingredients in general. The greatest expression of cuisine is when you don't have a lot of elements/ingredients per se and that you create something fabulous. You have to try to be in osmosis with the produce."

— Michel Bras

"I like to go out to eat for dinner when I have time off, see what other chefs are up to."

— David Burke

"There is less collaboration between chefs nowadays. I don't feel as though we are as united as we were. We used to have such a wonderful time. We were always partying."

— Paul Bocuse

"Cookery is not chemistry. It is an art. It requires instinct and taste rather than exact measurements."

— Marcel Boulestin

"Hopefully, imparting what's important to me, respect for the food and that information about the purveyors, people will realize that for a restaurant to be good, so many pieces have to come together."

— Thomas Keller

"I do not want guests walking out of the restaurant feeling as if they over-indulged because of excessive cream, butter and alcohol. I want them to feel stimulated and alert, knowing they will be able to look forward to breakfast the following morning."

— Charlie Trotter

"I like food that is simple and almost homely, that makes you feel comfortable, real food. I am less about food that looks very beautiful.... cooking to me is about finding the right ingredients. They are local but the taste I give them is global. It's about travelling and how I can take those foreign ingredients and make them feel my own. I like to keep everything fresh and honest."

— Stevie Parle

"The fun of the business is seducing diners and cultivating intimacy. At the end of the day I was happiest having that relationship with my guests,"

— David Bouley

"I opened my own restaurant when I was 17. I went broke, then traveled around the country, learning about different kinds of foods, had three other restaurants that went broke. It didn't all start just a few years ago!"

— Paul Prudhomme

"I believe in real food."

— Thomas Ferlesch

"When you find a waiter who is a waiter and not an actor, writer, musician or poet, you've found a jewel."

— Andre Soltner

"Few things are more beautiful to me than a bunch of thuggish, heavily tattooed line cooks moving around each other like ballerinas on a busy Saturday night. Seeing two guys who'd just as soon cut each other's throats in their off hours moving in unison with grace and ease can be as uplifting as any chemical stimulant or organized religion."

— Anthony Bourdain

"If neither of the two parties are happy, then you have a closed restaurant. And if only one of the two groups is happy, you have one that will close. So, to create an opportunity for both the customers and the staff to have a superior experience is my constant struggle."

— Mario Batali

"For a great meal or a great dining experience, many things must come together: the company, the mood, the setting, the food and of course the wine, all in harmony."

— Daniel Boulud

"I live in New York and I'm in New York basically all the time. I spend a lot of my time in my restaurants, and I feel like that's why they're successful."

— Bobby Flay

"Risk is to do something that 99 percent of the time would be a failure."

— Ferran Adrià

"I remember when I was in college, I used to watch Julia Child's cooking show during dinner and joke with my roommates about becoming a TV chef."

— Martin Yan

"If you work with me you will often be starting your day in the forest or on the shore because I believe foraging will shape you as a chef. I know it has shaped me. If you see how a plant grows and you taste it in situ you have a perfect example of how it should taste on the plate."

— René Redzepi

"Some of the things I think I learned from that were very educational as far as just paying bills — the basics in dealing with a restaurant like that. It was just life — the education involved in running the organization, even on a small level."

— Todd English

"I think the most wonderful thing in the world is another chef. I'm always excited about learning new things about food."

— Paul Prudhomme

"A jazz musician can improvise based on his knowledge of music. He understands how things go together. For a chef, once you have that basis, that's when cuisine is truly exciting."

— Charlie Trotter

"It's a very, very difficult space to operate in, the restaurant kitchen — it requires a lot of human beings to intersect at just the right place to make it all work out."

— Rocco DiSpirito

"Buy the best you can find or afford and don't overmanipulate it. If I cook a scallop, the best praise you can give me is that it tastes like a scallop."

— Tom Colicchio

"When you're a chef, you graze. You never get a chance to sit down and eat. They don't actually sit down and eat before you cook. So when I finish work, the first thing I'll do, and especially when I'm in New York, I'll go for a run. And I'll run 10 or 15k on my — and I run to gain my appetite."

— Gordon Ramsay

"As chefs, the power rests with us in terms of our buying decisions. So the more informed you are as a chef, the better chef you're going to be in the future. To create a recipe today or into the future is going to require a lot more than just weighing your ingredients. I think that a recipe in the future is going to be about what your ingredients mean in terms of how they're being grown, who's growing them, where are they coming from, how far did they travel."

— Dan Barber

"I firmly believe that the era of the tyrant chef screaming at everyone in the kitchen and everything done his way or the highway — is over."

— Tom Colicchio

"When I was a child, our whole family cooked. All my cousins cooked. All my aunts and uncles cooked. It was part of our heritage."

— Mario Batali

"My grandfather was a chef for a Baron in Sicily before he came to America. I grew up with him. I used to do my homework at one end of the kitchen table while he cooked at the other end."

— Vincent Schiavelli

"I more try to focus energy on making my food taste better. I'm very meticulous in execution. But, I operate in a spontaneous way; I like to put things together on the spot."

— Shea Gallante

"I'm a chef, and chefs are a little like rock stars. For the first day of summer, I dye my hair blonde, like Pamela Anderson-blonde. And then when the blonde is gone I get the fauxhawk. I like to change things up. I know the pink scarf, fauxhawk thing is not really American masculine, but I'm Italian, so I don't give a damn."

— Fabio Viviani

"In every one of my dishes, something has to be very comforting and familiar, but then there has to be an aspect of excitement and difference. We take normal ingredients, but we're taking them at the height of their season and then we're showcasing them in a unique fashion."

— Curtis Duffy

"Don't touch my dick, don't touch my knife."
— Anthony Bourdain

"Now the restaurants have begun to catch up with the wine-making; there are numerous great restaurants in Napa Valley, and it's wonderful because the people are there for just that — great food and great wine."
— Thomas Keller

"The fancy stuff, that's for amateur chefs. They need gadgets. I have 50 or 60 knives and I use just one."

— André Soltner

"I maintain standards and I strive for perfection. That level of pressure is conveyed in a very bullish way and that's what cooking is all about."

— Gordon Ramsay

"Cooking is an art and patience a virtue. Careful shopping, fresh ingredients and an unhurried approach are nearly all you need. There is one more thing — love. Love for food and love for those you invite to your table. With a combination of these things you can be an artist — not perhaps in the representational style of a Dutch master, but rather more like Gauguin, the naïve, or Van Gogh, the impressionist. Plates or pictures of sunshine taste of happiness and love."

— Keith Floyd

"I've long said that if I were about to be executed and were given a choice of my last meal, it would be bacon and eggs. There are few sights that appeal to me more than the streaks of lean and fat in a good side of bacon, or the lovely round of pinkish meat framed in delicate white fat that is Canadian bacon. Nothing is quite as intoxicating as the smell of bacon frying in the morning, save perhaps the smell of coffee brewing."

— James Beard

"There are things I wish I had known. One, how hard it really was. And two, that I should have gotten a business degree before a cooking degree."

— Jonathan Waxman

"The most important thing is to teach and to show them by example. You have to show a lot of love within one's work, so it will be passed onto the next generation."

— Paul Bocuse

"There used to be a lot of people in the business who didn't belong; today, they can't do that anymore. You have to be a professional who can deliver something good to the table."

— Jean-Georges Vongerichten

"Just like if you were brought up on a farm, you would most likely carry on your father's business as a farmer; I was brought up in the kitchen and ended up becoming a chef."

— Martin Yan

"You know the old adage that the customer's always right?" he said. "Well, I kind of think that the opposite is true. The customer is rarely right. And that is why you must seize the control of the circumstance and dominate every last detail: to guarantee that they're going to have a far better time than they ever would have had if they tried to control it themselves."

— Charlie Trotter

"My inspiration when I was a kid was my mother. Like many kids, my mother was quite a good home cook. And I liked that. At this time we had to be at school until we were fourteen. At fourteen we stopped school. So what do you do? I liked to cook. So, I said to my parents "I'd like to be a Chef."

— André Soltner

"To me, life without veal stock, pork fat, sausage, organ meat, demi-glace, or even stinky cheese is a life not worth living."

— Anthony Bourdain

"Slicing a warm slab of bacon is a lot like giving a ferret a shave. No matter how careful you are, somebody's going to get hurt."

— Alton Brown

"I have a very modern way of thinking; the chef is there to lead the team and not just to sit behind the piano."

— Alain Ducasse

"The discovery of a new dish does more for the happiness of mankind than the discovery of a star."

— Anthelme Brillat-Savarin

"I equate [being the chef] to a conductor conducting an orchestra. The conductor is the one
who's getting billing. You don't expect the conductor to jump in and start playing the instruments. In fact, if he does, you're in trouble.
Same thing with a chef."

— Tom Colicchio

"A chef who chases fame is totally egocentric, and in that sense it does affect the customer because that person is not taking care of the customer. He doesn't give that customer his due in terms of time and effort for the money that the customer pays."

— Jacques Pépin

"The bad part about being recognized is that when I walk into a restaurant and sit down, I've got to eat everything on the plate, whether it's good or bad. People would take it as an insult if I did otherwise."

— Paul Prudhomme

"Public and private food in America has become eatable, here and there extremely good. Only the fried potatoes go unchanged, as deadly as before."

— Luigi Barzine

"I want to run a proper kitchen with a pair of bollocks... it's high pressure, high energy and more importantly, real. That's how we keep it every day."

— Gordon Ramsay

"Desserts are like mistresses. They are bad for you. So if you are having one, you might as well have two."

— Alain Ducasse

"I typically start my day at 6 a.m. and work until noon or take a nap, and then go out and check one of my restaurants to make sure they're doing well, then go to bed around midnight. It's the double shift of a chef; it's a curse."

— Michel Mahe

"It's a misconception that chefs are rich. Some are, and goddamn it, they deserve it. And our business is growing. But did I get into this business to make money? No. Anyone who gets into this business to become rich and famous is a fucking moron."

— David Chang

"The objective is to achieve a comfort level between the cook/artist/performer and the customer/viewer/diner. And if we can achieve that, and the customers are happy and the cooks are happy, then we have a great experience."

— Mario Batali

"I'm meticulous about tasting everything at the restaurant, so I taste all the preparations before lunch and dinner. That means tasting around 50 dishes twice. There are times when I think I can't taste another thing."

— Rick Bayless

"There are trillions of different possibilities of combinations in food. Where will you start? That's what we think of as the mental palette."

— Ferran Adrià

"Vegetarians, and their Hezbollah-like splinter faction, the vegans .... are the enemy of everything good and decent in the human spirit."

— Anthony Bourdain

"Let's face it: if you and I have the same capabilities, the same energy, the same staff, if the only thing that's different between you and me is the products we can get, and I can get a better product than you, I'm going to be a better chef."

— Thomas Keller

"It is interesting to imagine that 20 or 30 years ago Japanese food was disliked and, today, 8 or 10 years old children prefer a sushi bar to McDonald's. This acceptance of international cuisine is explained by the fact that we are a young culture, open to multiple influences."

— Alex Atala

"Everyone's opening up these fucking farm-to-table bullshit restaurants. How else are you supposed to cook? You're supposed to get the best ingredients possible. Do you want a pat on the back?"

— David Chang

"Once you understand the foundations of cooking — whatever kind you like, whether it's French or Italian or Japanese — you really don't need a cookbook anymore."

— Thomas Keller

"Cuisine has become too complicated. This is about subject, verb, adjetive: duck, turnips, sauce."

— Alain Ducasse

"My passion comes from being able to create on the fly."

— Bobby Flay

"Maybe the Beatles can look back and say everything was perfect, but we've come up with hundreds and hundreds of dishes, and anyone who is honest with themselves has to realize that every single one wasn't an absolute, unequivocal home run."

— Wylie Dufresne

"If you can eat with mates or friends or family, I mean, it's such a brilliant thing isn't it? If you feel really rubbish and you have a nice bit of food it makes you feel good, you know?"

— Jamie Oliver

"If you don't have a humble attitude about food, then you'll be dead."

— Ferran Adrià

"Cooks have to ask yourselves, how bad do you want this? Life and death is what it means to me."

— David Chang

"Energy and passion define my style."

— Daniel Boulud

"You want to work with the food you want to do, but vibe is important, too. If it's total chaos every single day, it's going to wear on you after a while."

— Andrew Carmellini

"I work in collaboration with my sous chefs and we all are passionate about food. We all go to different restaurants, visit different markets, and are approached by farmers who bring new products. We explore new techniques and very often I say I would like to see what we can do with that technique and this ingredient, for instance, and let's see what comes out of it. Then, in collaboration we go to the next level where we are like, can we do a dish with that?"

— Eric Ripert

"My own food is a lot of times just stuff that looks at me and tells me what to do with it. I never went to cooking school, so I didn't really get professionally trained. And I just start remembering what my mother taught me about complementing the product."

— David Bouley

"Feeding people is by definition a repetitious act. Trying to make it perfect is what gives it meaning."

— Paul Liebrandt

"The way you make an omelet reveals your character."

— Anthony Bourdain

"The duty of a good cuisinier is to transmit to the next generation everything he has learned and experienced."

— Fernand Point

"When you have made as many mistakes as I have then you can be as good as me."

— Wolfgang Puck

"Knowing about 90% of your customers every night is the dream of every restaurateur. If you know what they like, you can make them happy. It's like strangers visiting in your house, you're not sure what they like, or what they don't like. But when you cook for people you know, you can keep building a higher level of pleasure, and that's what we want to get back to."

— David Bouley

"We [chefs] don't eat dinner. It's just impossible. From about 6.30 to 10.30 you're tasting, tasting, tasting, seeing your dishes on the menu. Going to the kitchen and wanting to taste what the customer is experiencing is crucial."

— Gordon Ramsay

"The restaurant industry is brutal."

— René Redzepi

"All the little increments of steps a cook takes, and changes that food goes through when executed correctly, are what make a good cook. The little things will help you gain a higher intuitive sense for cooking."

— Carmen Quagliata

"Spice is life. It depends upon what you like... have fun with it. Yes, food is serious, but you should have fun with it."

— Emeril Lagasse

"What I've enjoyed most, though, is meeting people who have a real interest in food and sharing ideas with them. Good food is a global thing and I find that there is always something new and amazing to learn."

— Jamie Oliver

"My inspiration comes from so many different things. If you're creating that many new dishes you can't only be inspired by great produce. It comes from many directions. You have to train your brain to find inspiration from everything"

— Heinz Beck

"For me, there's no better way to expose your-self to food than to travel. For me, food is an imprint of a culture. It allows you to try to understand what that culture's all about. I really enjoy understanding the psyche of the people via food as the vehicle. I'm not going to a country to go to their most critically acclaimed restaurants to take food from there and translate it back to me. I'm going to, basically, try and see what the soul of their food is and try and translate that."

— Michael Psilakis

"Everyone does it with a smile. And cooking is a subject you can never know enough about. There is always something new to discover."

— Bobby Flay

"I maintain standards and I strive for perfection. That level of pressure is conveyed in a very bullish way and that's what cooking is all about."

— Gordon Ramsay

"The bottom line you still have to make sense of what you do operationally and financially. You can't just have a restaurant where you just express yourself — this is who I am and this is what I do. If you don't like it then the hell with you... That is kind of utopian."

— Luciano Pellegrini

"I maintain standards and I strive for perfection. That level of pressure is conveyed in a very bullish way and that's what cooking is all about."

— Gordon Ramsay

"When I got out of school I told myself:
"School gave me a tool kit – not just a set of
knives – but a set of resources and skills that I
have to go out and develop." So I put my
head down and kept moving forward."

— Shea Gallante

"When it comes to cooking, that respect is paid to Mother Nature. That's first and foremost, anything else that's added or anything that's altered with a natural ingredient is done so slightly and with such reason. I find that cooking to be very elemental, and I really strive to prepare food that way. "

— Josh DeChellis

"Anybody can make you enjoy the first bite of a dish, but only a real chef can make you enjoy the last."

— Francois Minot

"If you aren't nervous about your passion, you aren't passionate about it."

— Bobby Flay

"Cooking evokes lots of feelings. The pleasure we get from doing our shopping is essential to the feeling that we are going to give to the dishes that we prepare."

— Alain Ducasse

"Let things taste of what they are."

— Alice Waters

"We may be three thousand miles and twelve blocks off Broadway, but what we do here is definitely theatre. We work hard to ensure that each evening's 'performance' is seamless and magical."

— Gary Danko

"I have a very classical style, French and German, and cook at a classical level. But at the artisanal level, I interpret this in my own way which is new and different. I reinterpret the cuisine and create new forms and structures. I like to play with spices in a well-balanced way with one, two or three components on the plate which participate in an interplay of different structures and aromas. I present things in a new way, but am still cooking at a very classical level. I don't do molecular cooking. Of course I allow myself to be influenced by new elements, but I don't become dominated by them. Rather the ingredients themselves are the star and stand in the foreground. The product dominates the plate and not its expression."

— Soren Anders

"I don't like the term 'dinner as theater,' because that implies something thespian that I don't want to tie into this, but there are plenty of times that people go out to dinner because they want to have an experience."

— Wylie Dufresne

"The chef's greatest achievement is to interfere as little as possible, while giving everything a sort of magic twist — the magic personal twist."

— Jeremiah Tower

"I believe that if ever I had to practice canni-
balism, I might manage if there were enough
tarragon around."

— James Beard

"I just think my job is not only as a chef, but
as a human being, and giving back. I think
eating locally is one way of supporting the
earth and the area, which is very important."

— Bill Telepan

"The best place to invent and create is in the kitchen. You can't paint without paint. I don't think every dish has to be a high-wire act, but there should be some personal touches.
I don't want to do something like everybody else."

— David Burke

"I always look at the fascination of diners coming through from the dining room into the kitchen — you can never get them out because they're just totally amazed at what's going on — sort of the air traffic control of the kitchens."

— Gordon Ramsay

"I convinced people that you could have a great restaurant that was simple, and that you should make your menu from the marketplace — every day."

— Jeremiah Tower

"One of the greatest pleasures of my life has been that I have never stopped learning about good cooking and good food."

— Edna Lewis

"I believe first in the quality of ingredients, local purchasing and in cooking seasonally. I also think it's really important for food to make sense and have a sense of place. It's clear when a dish went through an uninformed creative process, when it hasn't really been inspired by original, nostalgic, congruent thought."

— Zak Pelaccio

"Typical French kitchens, where I trained, are war zones, but I've found it hard to work passionately with that kind of conflict."

— Alfred Portale

"Cook ingredients that you are used to cooking by other techniques, such as fish, chicken, or hamburgers. In other words be comfortable with the ingredients you are using."

— Bobby Flay

"I like to fish. And listen to music. I like to bring music home to relax. After talking to people all day long in the restaurant, which I love to do, I look forward to being quiet at home."

— Emeril Lagasse

"I think in terms of creating food, it's a lot about creating food that you believe in, not just putting things together for the sake of putting things together."

— Dan Kluger

"I've long believed that good food, good eating, is all about risk. Whether we're talking about unpasteurized Stilton, raw oysters or working for organized crime 'associates,' food, for me, has always been an adventure."
— Anthony Bourdain

"I equate [being the chef] to a conductor conducting an orchestra. The conductor is the one who's getting billing. You don't expect the conductor to jump in and start playing the instruments. In fact, if he does, you're in trouble. Same thing with a chef."

— Tom Colicchio

"Ninety-nine percent of what you do will be failures, but someone has to take risks."

— Ferran Adrià

"When I'm hiring a cook for one of my restaurants, and I want to see what they can do, I usually ask them to make me an omelette."

— Bobby Flay

"People are really surprised how fragile restaurants are. You have to really keep on top of the game with the best food and best prices."

— Jean-Georges Vongerichten

"When I first decided to open a restaurant, I was turned down by several banks. It was the late 80's and many restaurants were failing. I refused to give up because I knew I had a good concept."

— Emeril Lagasse

"When things are seasonal and local, they taste better. When a carrot is pulled out of the ground that day from less than 100 miles away, it's going to taste better than a carrot that was pulled out of the ground a week ago and flown in from another part of the country."

— Bill Telepan

"Simple food is the stuff that is and always will be what people migrate to. Trends don't last at all. Cook simply, garden to plate, stop dissecting things and thinking they are so difficult. Roast a chicken perfectly, make a simple pasta, and you will unlock everything you need to know about cooking."

— Marc Vetri

"It's hard work to secure produce from soil to table and with this philosophy comes lot of trail and error."

— Björn Frantzén

"We are 'chef chefs,' the people who make this food revolution possible and bring the goodness of the earth right to our table."

— José Andres

"It's an ancestral method in Japan. Food preparation is a spectacle considered an integral part of the meal."

— Eiichi Edakuni

"I run my restaurant as a club so it's like cooking for friends. We know every diner by name, their favorite table and food."

— Anton Mosimann

"The fact that I do things the way I do them, that the food looks beautiful, has nothing to do with how approachable it is. In order to be approachable you have to lower your standards? No, not at all."

— Paul Liebrandt

"Everyone tries to compare cooks to rock stars. I see more comparisons to the fashion world. In fashion, you have one to two to three designers who actually do something new. Everyone else just fucking regurgitates and copies and steals and takes esoteric ideas from 20 or 30 years ago. And when there is something better, not everyone embraces it."

— David Chang

"A signature dish for me is one I create in my own style with a product I love."

— Dominique Bugnand

"Food must satisfy the eyes before it can appease the palate, so I strive to create a 'wow' element in all my creations."

— Bakshish Dean

"My palate is simpler than it used to be. A young chef adds and adds and adds to the plate. As you get older, you start to take away."

— Jacques Pépin

"A lot of people call me a celebrity chef, but I don't think that I'm a celebrity. So I want to stay keeping just a chef. That's more comfortable."

— Masaharu Morimoto

"For food it's all about balance to me. It's balance on a dish and balance throughout the menu. I'm always thinking about something from the beginning all the way through to the end, like the way you would think of a symphony. The thing I find most disappointing in high-end restaurants is there can be a tendency to be too much about the process and manipulation of the product. I have a lot of passion for the actual ingredients."

— Naomi Pomeroy

"My food is a little different from that of most restaurants. I get a little bored with the food prepared by most restaurant chefs. I have an enormous passion for real food like the food that is prepared at home. After all, the best meals are those made by someone you love, for you, the person they love."

— Reed Hearon

"The chef is simply a spoke in the wheel of the food cycle, a conduit for ingredients to get to the diner. We try to get the best things we can, try not to over manipulate them, and pass them along to a hungry audience."

— Beau Vestal

"There's a big difference between a cook and a chef. A chef isn't always someone that knows how to cook. The chef is the chief, the boss of the kitchen who makes it run to the financial and management standards of the restaurant owner."

— Kevin Koebel

"I think a lot of times people design restaurants with flash in mind. I think you should design restaurants with function in mind. Make sure it's functional and works with what you're trying to accomplish. Design can come later."

— Bobby Flay

"I believe that one of the things that unites us is the will to make a modern, creative cuisine, but always to talk about our origins, our culture and our products."

— Alex Atala

"It's my belief that cooking is a craft. I think that you can push it into the realm of art, but it starts with craft. It starts with an understanding of materials. It starts with an understanding of where foods are grown."

— Tom Colicchio

"I don't consider myself a rock star chef, I really don't. I cook for a living and I try to help out as many people as I can in my life and that's all I care about. I don't care about the fame of television, I use to a lot."

— Robert Irvine

"Make sure that you love eating, not just cooking. If not, you should look for another profession."

— Tetsuya Wakuda

"When making pasta I learned what to leave out of the pasta dish. The noodle is the king of the dish. Don't put a bunch of ingredients in. Keep it simple."

— Mario Batali

"Because I'm a chef, I eat out frequently, so it's hard for me to control what I consume in terms of calories. But when I'm at home, I eat what my wife cooks for me. She works hard to avoid making foods that are high in calories and cholesterol, so most of the time, she makes vegetarian dishes."

— Masaharu Morimoto

"The worst food you'll ever eat will probably be prepared by a 'cook' who calls himself a 'chef.' Mark my words."

— Alton Brown

"If you want to become a great chef, you have to work with great chefs. And that's exactly what I did."

— Gordon Ramsay

"Taste is what brings customers back — taste and seasoning."

— Jacques Imperato

"Inspiration comes from new territory. Inspiration has to happen while you are at work. That is the true meaning of being creative."

— José Andres

"I believe the future is vegetables and fruits. They are so much more sexier than a piece of chicken... Let's compare a chicken breast, the best chicken breast from the best farm with a beautiful pineapple. Cut the pineapple, already the aromas are inundating the entire kitchen. Acidity. Sour after notes, touches of passion fruit."

— José Andres

"His [Charlie Trotter's] restaurant was just different. You could tell. People talked different. People worked differently. The atmosphere was different. The feel of the restaurant was different. The environment was different, and I just knew there was something about it, like it was serious. It was special."

— David LeFevre

"Cooking is a craft. It's like being a carpenter or a furniture maker. You want to start out and get taken under somebody's wing and learn that way."

— Marco Canora

"A microwave oven! I never had one. I don't know how it works."

— Andre Soltner

"The ultimate success is on the plate. Longevity of success requires fundamental work ethics. It is very hard to convince young chefs today, who are often more focused on becoming famous rather than becoming a great cook. They want everything too fast. It takes time."

— Gray Kunz

"Be humble, work hard, read everything you can get your hands on, and you can learn something from everyone around you."

— Anthony Amoroso

"There is a way of life that I think people are returning to and sort of learning how enjoyable it is to forage for your ingredients to build a meal. To go buy bread from the person who makes really good bread, then go to the market and get your vegetables and then go to your meat or fish monger... those processes are a way of living your life with a little more rhythm. That way of life slows us down a little bit and is good for everyone."

— Ben Ford

"You can have anything you want in life, but you have to sacrifice everything — your personal life, finances. Do you homework. When you're home, read and dine out. That's paramount. If you work 12 hours here, you then need to do your homework; go to farmers markets and talk to other chefs."

— Christopher Kearse

"Good bread is the most fundamentally satisfying of all foods; good bread with fresh butter, the greatest of feasts!"

— James Beard

"Great cooking is about being inspired by the simple things around you — fresh markets, various spices. It doesn't necessarily have to look fancy."

— G. Garvin

"It's not easy to create things that will bring pleasure. But if we can do that, then, yes, it's enough."

— Ferran Adrià

"You don't need a silver fork to eat good food."
— Paul Prudhomme

"My vision is to not only define food and cooking as an art, but to go back to the roots of cooking and showcase the process through a more simplistic, ethereal approach as an expression of life and living."

— Lorena Garcia

"Cook everything, whenever you get a chance. Eat everything, and keep notes. Keep your eyes open and know that everything you do, whether you get paid for it or not, is experience, and that's priceless."

— JoAnna Minneci

"Modern cooking is nothing other than certain chefs moving forward."

— José Andres

"Could you imagine people eating a painting — if they could introduce a painting into their bodies? It's probably the artist's dream, and we have the opportunity to do so."

— Ferran Adrià

"Close interaction with farmers and scientists can expose the chef to new flavors that can be used to delight diners."

— Rene Redzepi

"Try to leave the expectations of the restaurant and your ego at the front door and just focus on the individuals on a daily basis."

— Tomislav Martinovic

"If you get to a certain point in your career and people know who you are, and you have certain notoriety — you are an ambassador. No matter how you think about it. The best ambassador in the world is Alice Waters. She's going around the country, and around the world, talking about edible gardens and eating beautiful foods and celebrating farmers and all this stuff. It's a different role than cooking on the line and creating dishes, but it's kind of the same thing. It's just a different way of approaching it."

— Jonathan Waxman

"If you've got a chef who understands food, who understands the cooking process, who understands baking, who understands flavors and temperature, they're going to end up making better food. It's about paying attention."

— Andre Guerrero

"If you want to cook at home, cook at home. If you don't want to cook at home, that's why there's restaurants."

— Scott Conant

"I liked the energy of cooking, the action, the camaraderie. I often compare the kitchen to sports and compare the chef to a coach. There are a lot of similarities to it."

— Todd English

"It's like anything, if you start out working for somebody really good. I'd much rather have someone who worked for a year at Babbo or Le Bernardin than someone who's just finished three years of culinary school."

— Suzanne Goin

"Food should be fun."

— Thomas Keller

"It is important to experiment and endlessly seek after creating the best possible flavors when preparing foods. That means not being afraid to experiment with various ingredients."

— Rocco DiSpirito

"I tend towards complexity of simplicity. It's what I like and what I'm looking for in my dishes. Respect my guests, my staff, my chefs, everything. We try to be all together and do things as well as we can."

— Sergi Arola

"Gone are the days where a restaurant that's open thirteen services a week sees a head chef in the kitchen every service."

— Brett Graham

"I think cooking all together is shooting from the hip — a little bit of planning, but it's all kind of in the moment when stuff comes in that inspires me. It's when practice meets opportunity, that's what all my training is. And I love simple American flavors."

— Adam Evans

"For me the philosophy of freedom and cross-breeding has kept developing with the different encounters of my travel. Initially, freedom and crossbreeding for me was the 6 different seasons of France that allowed me to grow different vegetables and fruits; the freshness and the varieties of each season, the zucchini and the 100 different breeds of tomatoes by mixing one with another. Later, I rediscovered freedom with my love for travel, as I learned the different culinary arts of different countries and crossbreeding them with French cuisine."

— Daniel Hebet

"Seventy percent of running a restaurant is a staff issue. These are very talented guys but it's important for them to learn discipline so they stay focused."

— Marcus Samuelsson

"Everything I do is from scratch. I've been doing organic for 14 years. I started with a hog farmer to make andouille sausage. In order to have great cuisine you need to have great ingredients."

— Emeril Lagasse

"La bonne cuisine est la base du véritable bonheur. (Good food is the foundation of genuine happiness)."

— Auguste Escoffier

"Food is our common ground, a universal experience."

— James Beard

"Once a year I ask some lamas, which are Tibetan monks in Nepal and in India, to do a ceremony, which is lighting a thousand lamps. It's an offering to the soul of the animals that we have killed and served at the restaurant."

— Eric Ripert

"My family truly believes they are better cooks than I am. They see me as Giada, not as a celebrity chef. To them I'm just me, their granddaughter, niece, etc., and they're older and wiser. I like that because it keeps you grounded."

— Giada De Laurentiis

"I think with food success is really about popularity. If nobody is eating it then you can't be a success. Even weird food gets eaten."

— Adam Fleischman

"Like most chefs or people in the business, you have some frenetic energy inside you all the time."

— Andrew Carmellini

"My philosophy from day one is that I can sleep better at night if I can improve an individual's knowledge about food and wine, and do it on a daily basis."

— Emeril Lagasse

"I think the conception part of cooking, the creative aspect of starting everything from scratch, is what I enjoy most and that's what I've been able to focus on. It keeps me from getting bored."

— Jeremy Fox

"I think every chef, not just in America, but across the world, has a double-edged sword — two jackets, one that's driven, a self-confessed perfectionist, thoroughbred, hate incompetence and switch off the stove, take off the jacket and become a family man."

— Gordon Ramsay

"As a chef, you need to respect your guests and their needs. If they decide that they want to eat certain things and not eat others, if for religious reasons or just decide they don't want to eat certain ingredients, you have to respect that."

— Joel Robuchon

"What I've enjoyed most, though, is meeting people who have a real interest in food and sharing ideas with them. Good food is a global thing and I find that there is always something new and amazing to learn."

— Jamie Oliver

"I liked the energy of cooking, the action, the camaraderie. I often compare the kitchen to sports and compare the chef to a coach. There are a lot of similarities to it."

— Todd English

"Slicing a warm slab of bacon is a lot like giving a ferret a shave. No matter how careful you are, somebody's going to get hurt."

— Alton Brown

"I'm never satisfied with what I do. I'm always hyper self-critical. I think that's what drives me along. Like a person who makes fried chicken and makes it the same way every time; that's boring to me. How can you be satisfied with that?"

— Jonathan Waxman

"You have no choice as a professional chef: you have to repeat, repeat, repeat, repeat until it becomes part of yourself. I certainly don't cook the same way I did 40 years ago, but the technique remains. And that's what the student needs to learn: the technique."

— Jacques Pépin

"I don't believe that I have any hard and true philosophies about food other than the fact that I believe that people should gather together in a place, enjoy each other's company and enjoy a good meal. They should savor the entire experience."

— John Manion

"Spice is life. It depends upon what you like... have fun with it. Yes, food is serious, but you should have fun with it."

— Emeril Lagasse

"Even if the chef has a good business head, his focus should be behind kitchen doors. A business partner should take care of everything in front of the kitchen doors."

— Bobby Flay

"I don't like to sit still for long at all, which has probably helped me along the way, and partly why I was drawn to the heat of a restaurant kitchen. The rush of service means that you're always on your toes and keeps a chef pretty active."

— Curtis Stone

"In France, formality is on the way out, so that it is now possible to have fun in restaurants. Chefs are not worried about silver forks anymore; they want to just cook and have fun."

— Pascal Barbot

"There are all kinds of myths going on in the Italian culture, and the way they celebrate is through their food. It's the tradition of the table where the Italians celebrate most of their triumphs and successes."

— Mario Batali

"The whole experience has to be about the food, the wine, the atmosphere – because it's about an all round experience. Everything has to be perfect."

— Roger Jones

"Some of the old-fashioned chefs, they become kings in their kitchen, they've got to be called chef. But I don't care if someone calls me chef or Heston, it really doesn't bother me."

— Heston Blumenthal

"Culinary school is not going to make you a chef but it's going to give you the basic techniques to get an entry level position in a restaurant. I think that is important for people to understand. You don't become a chef the day you graduate culinary school. It just gives you the opportunity to work in a restaurant at entry level. Then, like any other profession, you learn your skills in school and hone them in the field. You go work for chefs you think are terrific and spend a bunch of years doing that. To me, there's no magic to it. It's got to be a slow, steady process and it takes a long time."

— Bobby Flay

"The thing that I admire most about the French are the clients and the people themselves and their love for the table. They make time to eat. It's very admirable. They're not afraid to eat food that's so called bad for you. They're not afraid of dairy, they're not afraid of high fat items like foie gras. And they eat it. Everybody eats it. They eat a breakfast, they eat a lunch and they eat a dinner. They have a certain sense of moderation. They don't eat too much food. They don't seem to snack too. They eat on a regular basis and I think this regularity has a certain. You don't see a lot of overweight Frenchmen."

— David Kinch

"My main goal has always been to produce wonderful great food that's nutritious, that's tastefully done. Also, my other goal is to make every meal perfect."

— Bradley Ogden

"A chef making an entrée, is more in a "spirit of the moment"— tasting, reducing, figuring out how the dish comes together and playing with flavors."

— Hubert Keller

"Keeping it simple in my mind is that you get these great products from the farmers and you try to enhance it enough to bring out the natural characteristics of it. That's very important to me. It can be as complicated or as simple as you want it to be. If you use a product in it's natural state and just work with it and enhance it, I think you're better off."

— Bradley Ogden

"I think the chef on television has a lot of roles. They need to be a good teacher; they need to be able to inspire people; they need to be entertaining. In a lot of ways chefs on television are becoming role models for adults and children."

— Bobby Flay

"To be the best, you must work and work, and then work some more."

— Georges Perrier

"I was a musician for a long time, and I really think the reason musicians live long and interesting lives is that they just love what they do. And I think cooking is the same way. You won't become rich, but you'll be happy."

— Jonathan Waxman

"You're better off peeling potatoes at a great kitchen than working saucier at a really mediocre place."

— David Chang

"The difference between a rather average cook and a chef is that the chef is never really satisfied with what he is serving. He is constantly trying to achieve the high expectation he has set for himself. He is seeking to develop his palate and to enhance the skills of his palate through cooking, travel, and just being open. By keeping yourself open to what's new or who's doing something a little bit better, you strive for perfection. I'm always looking to improve on what I do."

— Bradley Ogden

CPSIA information can be obtained at www.ICGtesting.com
Printed in the USA
BVOW05s1845010514

352312BV00016B/440/P

9 781497 581975